Juliana Zen

We Can Be Better Tomorrow

Juliana Zen

We Can Be Better Tomorrow

The Effectiveness of Cognitive Training

ScienciaScripts

Imprint

Cover image: www.ingimage.com

This book is a translation from the original published under ISBN 978-620-2-03628-3.

Publisher:
Sciencia Scripts
is a trademark of
Dodo Books Indian Ocean Ltd. and OmniScriptum S.R.L publishing group

120 High Road, East Finchley, London, N2 9ED, United Kingdom
Str. Armeneasca 28/1, office 1, Chisinau MD-2012, Republic of Moldova, Europe
Managing Directors: Ieva Konstantinova, Victoria Ursu
info@omniscriptum.com

Printed at: see last page
ISBN: 978-620-8-52752-5

SUMMARY

SUMMARY

This study seeks to show, through scientific research, that brain stimulation programs can cooperate effectively in the regulation of psychopathologies, through structural and functional modification of the central nervous system, slowing down, halting or compensating for cognitive decline. The choice of this topic stems from the importance of encouraging the use of cognitive training in patients with brain disorders or injuries, given that brain plasticity is scientifically proven. This topic is discussed on the basis of exploratory research through a bibliographical review of the literature, outlining the studies and research on the subject. The effectiveness of cognitive training is highlighted, given the central nervous system's ability to adapt to environmental changes, offering an effective perspective for improving patients' quality of life. This study proves that we are in a new era when it comes to diagnosing and rehabilitating diseases involving the brain.

Keywords: Cognitive Training; Brain Plasticity; Cognitive Decline.

1. INTRODUCTION

As a result of research and studies, science already knows that the brain is extremely adaptable and can remodel itself according to an individual's experiences, a capacity called brain plasticity.

According to Goldberg (2011), the brain is malleable and has the capacity to function healthily, warding off illness and ageing, depending on how it is treated, what is done to it or not. According to Goldberg (2011), it is possible to alter the brain through a variety of cognitive exercises. According to him, in the same way that we work on the body in the gym, we can shape the brain through mental activity (GOLDBERG, apud, HUNTER, Andy, 2011).

There is a growing awareness of brain diseases and the search for an understanding of the neurological mechanisms involved in brain plasticity, the ability to replace damaged circuits with intact neighboring circuits, through cognitive and behavioral exercises.

Brain plasticity enables adaptation to changes in the environment, the storage of new information associated with learning, the reorganization of neural circuits in response to environmental stimulation, as well as recovery from injuries to the brain and spinal cord (Johnston, 2009 apud PORTO; OLIVEIRA; VOLCHAN; MARI; FIGUEIRA; VENTURA).

With this in mind, a group of researchers from Linkoping University, together with other Swedish universities, carried out a study with the aim of evaluating how cognitive behavioral therapy can affect brain volume and activity through cognitive training made available online. In this study, the researchers found that, in patients with Generalized Anxiety Disorder, brain volume and activity in the amygdala decreased as a result of cognitive behavioral therapy and the training carried out. It is worth noting that the amygdala is the brain structure responsible for states of fear, anger and aggression, symptoms present to varying degrees in individuals with Generalized Anxiety Disorder, one of the most common mental health problems. (SCIENCEDAILY, 2016).

According to Kristoffer NT Mansson (2016), the greater the improvement in patients' symptoms, the smaller the size of the tonsil, and this reduction in volume drives a reduction in brain activity. During the study, MRI scans were taken before and after treatment (SCIENCEDAILY, 2016).

Although it was a small sample, since the study was carried out with twenty-six individuals and lasted nine weeks, the research shows that patients can generate structural changes in their brains.

This study makes it clear that there is an exchange between cognitive behavioral therapy and neuroscience, allowing for a dialogue between mind and brain. We can consider that, although independent, mind and brain are integrated. Mental processes influence brain plasticity at various levels such as cellular, molecular and neural circuits (Beauregard, 2007 apud PORTO; OLIVEIRA; VOLCHAN; MARI; FIGUEIRA; VENTURA).

Brain plasticity shows the relationship established between the body and the environment and, therefore, the possibility of applying a cognitive rehabilitation program. It is therefore possible to eliminate or mitigate cognitive difficulties through a program of activities which stimulate various cognitive functions such as attention, memory, language and processing speed, contributing to the preservation or recovery of cognitive capacity.

Cognitive decline can be prevented, halted and even compensated for. Numerous tools have been developed as therapeutic resources in cognitive stimulation programs. Websites, clinics and even so-called gyms are multiplying, all focusing on brain exercises.

Neuroscientist Miguel Nicolelis, who coordinated the *Walk Again Project*, reports on the results obtained with the exoskeleton project, which was publicly demonstrated at the opening of the World Cup in Brazil in 2014, where the first kick of the ball was taken by a paraplegic wearing a motorized exoskeleton connected to his brain.

According to the neuroscientist, after a year of training with the eight paraplegic patients involved in the project who followed the training with the brain-controlled system, including a motorized exoskeleton, they regained the ability to move their leg muscles voluntarily and to feel touch, and even pain, in their paralyzed limbs. It is worth noting that these patients were initially diagnosed with a complete spinal cord injury, in some cases more than ten years ago. In addition, there has been improvement in organs such as the bladder, intestines and heart function (NICOLELIS, Miguel. 2017).

The researchers involved in the project point to the likelihood that the training promoted brain reorganization by activating latent nerves that may have survived the spinal cord injury (NICOLELIS, Miguel. 2017).

This discovery will certainly change rehabilitation practices for patients with spinal cord injuries from now on.

Generally speaking, it can be said that this is a recent area of study which has not yet been widely publicized, and it is a great challenge to investigate the proposed topic. The aim of this paper is therefore to discuss the extent to which cognitive stimulation plays a substantial role in empowering patients, helping them to overcome, reduce or overcome cognitive deficiencies and having an impact on their quality of life.

2. *OBJECTIVE*

The aim of this study is to research and demonstrate the effectiveness of using cognitive training to stimulate brain plasticity.

2.1 Specific Objectives

a) To encourage the use of cognitive training in the psychotherapeutic process with patients who have cognitive decline as a result of brain disorders or injuries.
b) Offering the prospect of improved quality of life for patients and relatives of those with brain disorders or injuries.

3. METHODOLOGY

3.1 Bibliographic survey

This study will be based on exploratory research through a literature review. In order to delineate the existing knowledge on the subject, the research will be carried out on articles published in national and foreign magazines, scientific journals and dissertations on the subject. The study will use *Scielo, Pubmed* and Dominio Publico as the basis for the bibliographic survey.

The definition of key words for the bibliographical survey will focus on the combination of the following expressions: (cognitive training and/or brain plasticity).

The inclusion criteria will be Portuguese or English; case studies on the use of cognitive training and its results in neuropsychological rehabilitation , and articles published between 2011 and 2017. After surveying the existing articles in these databases using the keywords, those that fall outside the scope defined in the project will be discarded.

The selected articles and materials that meet the main contributions according to the interest of the research will be read and summarized in order to contextualize and justify the research, as well as supporting the subsequent data analysis.

3.2 Data Collection Procedures

Having carried out bibliographic research: in newspapers, magazines, as well as other publications, with data related to the subject of this empirical study, the aim is to discuss and highlight the benefits of cognitive training in the recovery of patients with neurological disorders or injuries, as a result of brain plasticity.

3.3 Data Analysis Procedures

The articles that make up the theoretical platform of

this research will be analyzed in a qualitative way, and classified according to the information and results that strengthen the object of this study.

Relevant evidence from data, opinions, information and case studies will be addressed and will underpin the proposed research. The data analysis will discuss the main interpretations and lines of argument, exposing the most significant aspects of this study.

4. RESULTS AND DISCUSSIONS

Based on the data collected, it is clear that brain plasticity allows the brain to learn permanently, from learning a new language to recovering certain functions in the face of brain injury. There are numerous reports in the literature, on the internet and in magazines about studies that show improvements in the quality of life of patients with dementia, anxiety and phobias, for example.

Yes, the brain promotes change based on repeated experiences. This ability of the brain to modify its structure based on repeated behaviors, emotions and thoughts is an exciting truth that has been gaining more and more focus over the last decade. These are new possibilities within everyone's reach.

Cognitive training, i.e. brain stimulation programs, can work effectively to regulate psychopathologies by modifying the structure and function of the central nervous system, slowing down, halting and even compensating for cognitive decline.

This study aims to encourage the use of

cognitive training in the psychotherapeutic process by offering patients with cognitive decline, as a result of disorders or brain damage, the latest therapeutic techniques. In addition, the use of cognitive training in healthy adult patients allows growth and development to be generated, delaying the expected symptoms of the ageing process.

Certainly, a case study would qualify this research even more, however, due to time constraints, it was not possible to follow up a patient in its entirety, thus restricting this study to exploratory research on the subject.

In 2013, then President Obama launched a "brain" initiative, encouraging researchers to seek treatment for a variety of brain disorders such as Alzheimer's, Schizophrenia, Autism, Eplepsy and Traumatic Brain Injury, given that the World Health Organization estimated at the time that brain disorders affect more than one billion people worldwide . (National Institutes of Health. 2016)

Neural plasticity or neuroplasticity refers to the ability to transform and adapt the structure and function of neurons in response to the external and internal demands of the organism.

Any experience that challenges the brain, for example learning to play tennis, produces very significant anatomical changes at the cellular level such as an increase in dendrites (filaments that branch out from the center of the cell to connect other neurons), an increase in the number of dendritic spines, formation of new synapses (which are the points of contact between neurons that transfer and store information), increased activity of neuroglia (non-neural cells in the central nervous system that provide support and nourishment to neurons) and changes in cell metabolism (chemical transformations). (MCKAY, Sarah. 2016)

According to Dr. Sarah McKay, there are four types of neuroplasticity. 1. synaptic neuroplasticity, which are several complex stages that allow the development of the brain containing more than 100 billion neurons (brain cells) interconnected by more than a trillion synapses. Synaptic neuroplasticity works by the addition or remapping of synapses, or by changing the strength or efficiency of synapses. 2. neurogenesis, which is the birth and integration of new brain cells into existing neural circuits. It is the birth of new neurons in the brain.

Adult neurogenesis occurs in the hippocampus, part of the limbic system that contributes to memory formation and emotional control. 3. cortical reorganization, which involves reorganizing the maps in the cortex that represent the body and the external world. With each new learning experience, the brain expands its neural connections, reorganizes itself and modifies its capacities, expanding them and fixing them in memory. 4) Myelination. Myelin (the so-called white matter of the brain) increases the speed at which signals are transmitted through the axon (responsible for the conduction of the electrical impulse), increasing the speed at which information is processed. Oligodendrocytes, brain cells that wrap myelin around axons, increase myelination, which **is** an important component of brain maturation because it facilitates the transmission of nerve impulses in the central nervous system, speeding up processing. (MCKAY, Sarah. 2016)

The power of neuroplasticity can be understood through habits. When we repeat thoughts or perform certain behaviors over and over again, new synapses are formed and existing synapses in specific brain circuits become more efficient and powerfully connected.

As the neural circuit strengthens, repeated thoughts or behaviors become ingrained and a habit develops. "Some neural circuits become so ingrained that we carry out the habit even when we are desperate not to," says Dr. Sarah McKay. At the same time, "if you practice and repeat a new behavior or thought, you can develop new positive habits," adds Dr. Sarah Mckay. (MCKAY, Sarah. 2016).

Just over three decades ago, scientists began to see the brain in a different light. According to Dr. Merzenich, studies show that the adult brain remains plastic and capable of changing chemically, physically and functionally, based on sensory inputs. Previously, it was believed that this capacity was restricted to childhood (GLOBE NEWS WIRE. 2017).

For many years, there was a consensus that the human brain could not generate new cells once it reached adulthood, initiating a process of neural decline.

At the beginning of the 1930s, Cajal, the founder of modern neuroscience, had a gloomy prognosis for adult brains, saying that "nerve pathways are something solved, finalized, immutable. Everything can die and nothing can be regenerated". (CAJAL apud ABRAMS,

Michael. WINTERS, Dan. 2013).

It wasn't until the 1960s that two pioneers, Paul Bach-y-Rita and Michael Merzenich, started talking about "future science". Bach-y-Rita is best known for his work that enabled blind people to "see" in a new and radically different way. Instead of receiving information about the world through their eyes, the patients received it in the form of vibrations on their skin.

The patients sat in a chair and leaned back on a sheet of metal. Underneath this sheet were plates that vibrated according to the way a certain object moved. People with congenital blindness began to report experiences of "seeing" in three dimensions. Over time, the Bach-y-Rita devices have become more sophisticated and the latest version is in the tongue.

However, it was only with the advent of diagnostic imaging technology that scientists began to see proof of this hypothesis. The information seemed to be being processed in the visual cortex.

The confirmation that the brain contains maps of the body and the outside world, and that these maps have the ability to change, reinforcing the principle of neuroplasticity, came at the end of the 1960s when

Merzenich developed the cochlear implant. The implant allowed deaf people to hear from an artificial implant and no longer from the cochlea, since the organ was no longer functioning. The brain needs to adapt to receive auditory information from the artificial implant instead of the cochlea. Based on these findings, Merzenich and Bach-y-Rita proved to the scientific community that Cajal's predictions were wrong, the adult brain is plastic. (MERZENICH, Michael apud ABRAMS, Michael. WINTERS, Dan. 2013)

In the adult brain, neuroplasticity generates and integrates new brain cells (neurons) and remodels pre-existing neural circuits. Everything that is thought, felt, experienced and done is transmitted through neural circuits in the brain. These same thoughts, feelings, experiences and supports have the ability to change and shape the very circuits through which they travel. In a sense, the mind and its mental states become the brain itself. According to Dr. Rick Hanson, "day after day, your mind is building your brain". Certainly young, developing brains do this more easily than older brains. (Hanson apud MCKAY, Sarah. 2016)

An interesting fact, observed in studies with older

people, was the revelation that the effects are greater when the training is of a shorter duration (one to six weeks) than when it is longer (seven to twelve weeks). Although this is a small sample, the finding has practical implications, as many intervention programs spend a large amount of time training older participants, on the assumption that longer training will produce better results. (BALLESTEROS, S.; Prieto, A.; MAYAS, J.; Toril, P.; PITA, C.; PONCE de Leon, L.; Reales J.M.; WATERWORTH, J. 2014)

The circuits in our brain change in response to all experiences, not only during development, but also after an injury, or during learning and memory formation. Neuroplasticity is a constant process that occurs throughout life. The areas of our brain associated with emotions and memories (the prefrontal cortex, amygdala and hippocampus) are particularly plastic. According to Eric Kandel "all forms of therapy, regardless of theoretical orientation, will be successful to the degree that they promote neural growth and integration". Cognitive training is therefore a viable means of generating lasting neuroplastic changes, as well as emotional and behavioral changes. (KANDEL. 1998)

Age-related memory loss represents a loss of self, affecting the practical side of life. It is not surprising, therefore, that concerns about declining thinking and memory skills are one of the main fears that people have as they get older. (DAFFNER, K. R.; ALLISON, K. C.; LEIGHTON, S. & LINKIHOKER, M. 2012)

The brain is constantly changing its structure, and this change can be for the better or for the worse. The advantage is that, through focused attention, we can direct the process of neuroplasticity to change our brain in a healthy and beneficial way, slowing down or halting cognitive decline, for example.

Dr. Sarah McKay's recent research demonstrates this brain construction. According to her, in certain circumstances, the power of brain plasticity can help adult brains to grow and develop. "Plasticity is activated in adulthood when specific conditions or certain triggers are met." Despite the tendency for brain activity to decrease with age, there are steps people can take to reinvigorate the brain. (MCKAY, Sarah. 2016)

Along these lines, the award-winning Dr. Merzenich has developed exercises to monitor and improve individual health and performance. Published and peer-reviewed articles show improvements in performance across a range of populations. Studies in healthy mature adults have shown gains in measures of standard and actual cognition (brain speed, attention, memory and executive function), quality of life (mood, confidence, self-rated health, functional independence), and daily activities (balance, movement, driving). The online exercises developed in apps by Dr. Merzenich can be accessed on Posit Science's BrainHQ brain-training platform (GLOBE NEWS WIRE. 2017).

Cognitive training focused on rehabilitation needs to encourage patients to seek new adaptive coping strategies by creating new neural circuits. It is necessary to get out of the comfort zone and train the brain to respond in a new and more effective way to challenges.

Cognitive training incorporates strategies and principles used in cognitive behavioral therapy, which helps patients reframe situations and learn more productive ways of dealing with them ; and the principles of positive psychology, a relatively new clinical slant that identifies and builds on people's strengths rather than trying to correct weaknesses. (MEDICAL HARVARD SCHOOL. 2010)

Based on the studies and experiences developed during cognitive training, Kleim and Jones proposed ten principles of brain plasticity and published the study as follows:

1. The use of neural networks is essential for maintaining functionality.
2. A brain function can be strengthened by training.
3. Depending on the training used, brain plasticity can be restricted to the function trained.
4. Plasticity occurs through repeated task training.
5. The intensity of training is a factor that must be observed in order to induce plasticity.
6. The closer to the post-injury period that cognitive rehabilitation begins, the greater the behavioral results and physiological response in the plasticity process. The time variable is therefore very important.
7. An attractive and engaging rehabilitation program should be offered to the patient so that the information is better codified.
8. Age is another variable to take into account, as the younger the individual, the easier it will be to stimulate brain plasticity.
9. The phenomenon of transference can occur when

stimulation of a certain neural substrate promotes improvements in other neural pathways. Training one skill acts as a facilitator for improving other skills.

10. The phenomenon of interference occurs when some areas of the brain are stimulated from interaction with the environment or artificially and prevent other areas from benefiting from the process. (KLEIM, Jefrey; JONES, Theresa. 2008)

The effectiveness of cognitive training is a fact. Numerous studies, research and projects prove this. The Exoskeleton project by Brazilian neuroscientist Miguel Nicolelis is a very current example. Getting paraplegic patients on their feet with the help of robots and the use of a brain-machine interface led the brain to release the process of brain reorganization, i.e. reorganize and reinsert the concept of walking where it had been eliminated.

When he started the project, Dr. Nicolelis would say to the patients, "Think that you are going to walk now, think that you are moving your legs". And nothing happened to the brain's electrical activity, which no longer registered the concept or representation of the legs. However, as recovery progressed, brain activity changed. "Today, when they imagine the movement of the legs, you see the brain activity modulating appropriately, a signal related to the movement is extracted," points out Dr. Nicolelis. (NICOLELIS, Miguel. 2017)

During the training sessions, the patient had to imagine that he was controlling his exoskeleton, his robot. They had to interpret the tactile sensation. "We created the illusion of the phantom limb," says Dr. Nicolelis, who goes on to say, "the patients reported that they were walking," even though they were standing still. (NICOLELIS, Miguel. 2017)

Research shows that in sixty percent of cases of injury, two to twenty percent of the spinal cord remains intact, i.e. there are nerves. Thus Dr. Nicolelis' work proves that some kind of recovery is possible through cognitive training, taking advantage of these remaining nerves.

The result of this work shows that the diagnosis for patients with spinal cord injury and paralysis is no longer a closed diagnosis. There are probably a large number of patients with the possibility of some kind of neurological recovery. (NICOLELIS, Miguel. 2017)

It has also been proven that the cognitive training of thinking about physical exercises strengthens muscles, even if you don't move an inch. Mental images activate the same brain regions that real movement would activate, and can also speed up the learning of a new skill, for example, playing golf.

This type of training is being used by Dr. Guang Yue and his team at the Kessler Foundation to help improve the muscular strength of patients undergoing rehabilitation. According to Dr. Yue "evidence suggests that cognitive training without physical or muscular exercise can improve voluntary muscle strength". This finding could have significant application in the rehabilitation process for debilitated or frail elderly patients who find it difficult to participate in conventional strength training, such as weightlifting programs, "now they can strengthen their muscles using their mind," says Dr. Yue. (YUE, Guang. 2017)

Other work is being carried out at the Kessler Foundation laboratory. The work on multiple sclerosis, for example, challenges the current view of the cause of memory impairment. Studies are showing that memory impairment in individuals with multiple sclerosis is due to a loss of information acquisition and not a failure in retrieval. Therefore, training is now focused on cognitive rehabilitation programs to treat learning and memory problems.

Kessler Foundation scientists are also investigating cognition in various populations to understand the impact on learning and memory impairments in individuals with neurological injuries or diseases. They are using rehabilitation techniques to improve learning and memory and investigating how executive skills and processing speed impact learning and memory. (YUE, Guang. 2017)

Jeff Brown, a cognitive behavioral psychologist at Harvard Medical School and Mark Fenske, a neuroscience researcher, through diagnostic imaging studies suggest that the way people use their minds can alter neural circuits and, in some cases, create brain tissue. One example is that of an airline pilot, who repeatedly acts out simulated emergency situations to prepare for the possibility of a crash landing. Several studies suggest that such repetitive practice in a particular task or skill can create brain tissue. (MEDICAL HARVARD SCHOOL. 2010)

Cognitive training can be tailored to different performance levels and profiles. It can be aimed at healthy adults or elderly people, those with mild cognitive impairment, those with early or advanced dementia, or those with brain damage. Training can also be tailored to the degree of existing impairment or with the intention of preventing its occurrence. (DAFFNER, K. R.; ALLISON, K. C.; LEIGHTON, S. & LINKIHOKER, M. 2012)

The cognitive training program stimulates various cognitive functions such as attention, memory, language, processing speed, among others. The training is designed to suit each person's cognitive profile and can be carried out using different resources, such as technology.

Brain stimulation programs can cooperate effectively in the regulation of psychopathologies by modifying the structure and function of the central nervous system, slowing down, halting and even compensating for cognitive decline.

This set of procedures and techniques, applied in an effort to improve the patient's functional quality in their daily life, is individualized and tailored to each patient's needs. It is based on the patient's cognitive, intellectual and social profile prior to the illness. Before defining the training, the impaired and preserved cognitive functions must be assessed, a personality profile must be examined and goals and resources to be worked on in the rehabilitation must be determined.

Although personalized, the techniques used for cognitive training are very similar in the studies. Instructional training focused on exercises to stimulate memory and language; spatial orientation, organization and action planning; compensatory techniques and strategies; relaxation and meditation. In many cases, more than one technique is used, showing that the tools can be used together, allowing them to be adapted to the case and the planned treatment.

Cognitive training as a clinical practice enables patients to make *progress* by minimizing symptoms and even eliminating them. Clinical models of assessment and intervention are being proposed and offer alternatives for cases of cognitive impairment due to ageing, disorders and brain injuries.

Certainly, advances in research and the application of innovative technologies will revolutionize our understanding of the brain. Researchers are looking for new ways to treat, cure and even prevent brain disorders, filling large gaps in our current knowledge and exploring how the brain allows the body to record, process, use, store and retrieve large amounts of information, all at the speed of thought. "In just three years, we've already seen exciting new advances in neuroscience research," says Dr. Walter Koroshetz, director of the National Institute of Neurological Disorders at the National Institutes of Health (National Institutes of Health. 2016).

Much more to come! According to Dr. Joshua Gordon, director of the National Institute of Mental Health at the National Institutes of Health, among what is being proposed are computer programs that can help detect and diagnose autism and Alzheimer's disease from brain scans; the construction of a bone that uses ultrasound waves to stimulate brain cells; studies of how the brain reads and speaks; new rehabilitation technologies for stroke patients, among others. "Some of these projects aim to fine-tune brain stimulation and other promising technologies for the treatment of mental illness," says Dr. Joshua Gordon. (National Institutes of Health. 2016)

The brain is certainly the most complex part of the

human body. It is responsible for our intelligence, interpreting sensation, initiating body movement and controlling all our behaviors. The ability to better treat, prevent and cure brain disorders depends on our ability to advance our understanding of how the brain works in both health and disease.

The human brain is the most complicated organ in the body - probably the most complicated and calculated machine we know. (LANDIS. 2016)

5. FINAL CONSIDERATIONS

The scientific consensus is that brain plasticity is the ability of the nervous system to adapt in response to environmental changes resulting from experience, behavior or some long-term brain injury, be it damage or dysfunction. It is the ability of the brain to reorganize itself physiologically and respond functionally. What's more, it accompanies neurological development throughout life.

Although the brain's processing speed tends to slow down with age, the brain remains plastic throughout life, forming new synaptic connections in response to new experiences and environmental challenges. The challenge is to make use of this innate gift that we have all been given.

For a long time it was almost universally accepted in the field of neuroscience that, once formed and structured, the adult brain did not manufacture any more neurons and only changed due to declining age.

Thanks to huge advances in diagnostic imaging and functional magnetic resonance imaging, we have a better understanding of how our brain works and have begun to discover fantastic capabilities and abilities that were previously unknown. I believe that the greatest recent discovery is the fact that the brain evolves continuously and is extraordinarily flexible. This discovery replaces the old belief that the brain after adulthood is a physiologically static organ.

Brain plasticity is the process that allows all permanent learning to take place, from learning to play chess to rehabilitation from cognitive loss due to injury. Neuroplasticity allows people to recover from strokes, injuries and congenital abnormalities, overcome learning difficulties, overcome depression, eliminate addictions and become better every day. And all this can be achieved through cognitive training exercises, individualized programs according to each patient's profile and conducted by qualified professionals.

We know, and studies show, that the brain is much more plastic during the first few years of life and as age progresses, it undergoes a decline in remodeling capacity, but plasticity occurs throughout life.

Studies have shown the effectiveness of cognitive

training and it has gained prominence among researchers around the world. The

genes are no longer the final destination. Culture, language, climate, nutrition, memories and thoughts allow the brain to change and improve on a daily basis.

Yes, we can grow old by making tomorrow better than today. Plasticity allows our brain to be more efficient every day. We can redirect our lives in search of growth and even rejuvenation, and I believe we are moving in this direction quite quickly. We are certainly facing a new era when it comes to diagnosing and rehabilitating diseases involving the brain.

Based on years of research, study and observations, we now know that the processes that allow us to recover from illness and injury are plasticity and adaptation. Plasticity, due to changes in the structure and physiology of the central nervous system. Adaptation, due to changes in the strategies that individuals use to perform tasks in new ways to overcome their disabilities.

Learning how to improve the brain's natural plasticity mechanisms is fundamental to developing more effective rehabilitation. Given the remarkable progress that has already been made and that is yet to come, I believe that we will not be surprised when we come across a quadriplegic individual parking his adapted car, guided only by the power of his thoughts.

Studies and research, and new discoveries in this area emerge day after day. It is up to health professionals to immerse themselves in this universe, seeking to offer the most up-to-date and demonstrably effective tools for the rehabilitation of their patients. Learning how to learn. We can all be better tomorrow.

BIBLIOGRAPHICAL REFERENCES

ABRAMS, Michael; WINTERS, Dan. Discover. **Can You See With Your Tongue?The Brain Is So Adaptable, Some Researchers Now Think, That Any Of The Five Senses Can Be Rewired.** US. 2003. Available at <http://discovermagazine.com/2003/jun/feattongue>. Accessed on: September 07, 2017.

BALLESTEROS S.; Prieto, A.; MAYAS, J.; Toril, P.; PITA, C.; PONCE de Leon, L.; Reales J.M.; WATERWORTH, J.. **Brain Training With NonAction Video Games Enhances Aspects of Cognition in Older Adults - A Randomized Controlled Trial. In: Front**. Aging Neuroscience. US. 2014. Available at: <https://www.ncbi.nlm.nih.gov/pmc/articles/PMC4196565 />. Accessed on: August 31, 2017.

CHARCHAT-FICHMAN, Helenice; SANTOS FERNANDES, Conceigao; FERNANDES, J. Landeira; **Neurocognitive Psychotherapy Behavioral: an Interface between Psychology and Neuroscience**. Rio de Janeiro. Vol. 8 no. 1. June 2012.

Available at <http://pepsic.bvsalud.org/scielo.php?script=sci_arttext& pid=S18085687 201200106> Accessed on: February 18, 2017.

CASTREN, Eero. **Induction of Neuronal Plasticity the Adult Brain: Mechanisms and Applications.** University of Helsinki. Finland. 2014.

Available at <http://www.helsinki.fi/neurosci/groups/castren.html>. Accessed on: August 14, 2017.

DAFFNER, K. R.; ALLISON, K. C.; LEIGHTON, S. & LINKIHOKER, M. **Improving Memory - Understanding Age-Related Memory Loss.** 1st ed. Boston: Medical Harvard School, 2012. Available at <https://www.health.harvard.edu/mind-and-mood/improving-memory- understanding-age-related-memory-loss>. Accessed on: August 31, 2017.

GLOBE NEWSWIRE. **A Road Map to How to Change**

Your Brain. San Francisco. Feb.2017. Available at <https://globenewswire.com/news-release/2017/02/21/926129/0/en/A- Road-Map-How-to-Change-Your-Brain.html>. Accessed on: August 29, 2017.

GORDON, Joshua. **National Institutes of Health - Turning Discovery Into Health**. Maryland. 2016. Available at <https://www.nih.gov/news-events/news-releases/nihnames-dr-joshua- gordon-directo -national-institute-mental-health>. Accessed on: September 1, 2017.

HUNTER, Andy. On The Threshold: An Interview With Elkhonon Goldberg, Ph.D. **International Brain Education Association**. New York. Mar. 2011. Available at <http://www.brainworldmagazine.com/>. Accessed on: August 14, 2017.

KANDEL, Eric. **The American Journal of Psychiatry. A New Intellectual Framework for Psychiatry.** US. 1998. Available at <https://doi.org/ 10.1176/aip.115.4.457>. Accessed on: September 06, 2017.

KLEIM, Jefrey; JONES, Theresa. **Journal of Speech, Language and Hearing Research.** Principles of Experience-Dependent Neural Plasticity: Implications for Rehabilitation After Brain Damage. US. Feb. 2008. Available at <https://jslhr.pubs.asha.org/article.aspx?articleid=1773394>. Accessed on: September 06, 2017.

KOROSHETZ, Walter. **National Institutes of Health Turning Discovery Into Health.** Maryland. 2016. Available at <https://www.braininitiative.nih.gov/?AspxAutoDetectCookieSupport=1>. Accessed on: September 1, 2017.

LANDIS, Story. **Advancing Our Understanding of the Brain**. US. Dec. 2016. Available at <http://www.braininitiative.org/>. Accessed on: September 1, 2017.

LUCENA, Eleonora. **Research Changes Paradigm for the Treatment of Paralysis, Says Nicolelis.** Folha Digital. Sao Paulo. 2016. Available at <http://www.1.folha.uol.com.br/ciencia/2016/08/1801617-

pesquisa-muda paradigma-for-the-treatment-of-paralysis-says-nicolelis.shtml>. Accessed on: August 12, 2017.

MCKAY, Sarah. **Your Brain Health**. **Discovery Neuroscience. Explore Brain.**

Understaind Your Mind. Oxford. 2016. Available at: <http://yourbrainhealth.com.au/>. Accessed on: August 30, 2017.

MCKAY, Sarah. **Your Brain Health**. **Can You Think Yourself Into a Different Person?** Oxford. 2015. Available at: <http://yourbrainhealth.com.au/can-you-think-yourself-into-a-different- person>. Accessed on: September 6, 2017.

MEDICAL HARVARD SCHOOL. **Cultivating a Winner's Brain.** ***Psychological Strategies that People can use to Improve Mental Performance.*** Boston. 2010. Available at <https://www.health.harvard.edu/newsletterarticle/cultivat

ing-a-winners- brain>. Accessed on: September 6, 2017.

NICOLELIS, Miguel.Laboratory of Miguel A. L.Nicolelis M.D.,PH.D. **Duque University Medical Center**. North Carolina. 2017. Available at <http://www. http://www.nicolelislab.net/?p=784>. Accessed on: August 14, 2017.

PORTO, Patricia; OLIVEIRA, Leticia; VOLCHAN Eliane; MARI Jair; FIGUEIRA Ivan; VENTURA Paula. **Scientific Evidence from Neuroscience for Cognitive Behavioral Therapy.** Paideia (Ribeirao Preto). Vol.18 no.41.2008. Available at <http://www.scielo.br/scielo.php?script=sci_arttext&pid=S 0103863X2 0 8000300006>. Accessed on: February 17, 2017.

SANZ SIMON, Sharon Sanz Simon; PIERRO DE OLIVEIRA RIBEIRO, Marilda. **Mild Cognitive Impairment and Neuropsychological Rehabilitation**. Sao Paulo. Vol.20 n.1. 2011. Available at <http://www.revistas.pucsp.br/index.php/articl

/viewFile/6795/491>. Accessed on: August 14, 2017.

SCIENCEDAILY. **Brain Volume Changes After Cognitive Behavioral Therapy.** Rokville. Feb. 2016. Available at <https://www.sciencedaily.com/releases/2016/02/160202185552.htm?>. Accessed on: February 18, 2017.

VIEIRA MACHADO, Rodrigo. **Journal of Clinical Psychiatry**. Vol.40 no.3. Sao Paulo. 2013. Available at < http://www. scielo.br/scielo.php?pid=S010160832013>. Accessed on: August 12, 2017.

YUE, Guang. **Kessler Foundation. Neuropsychology & Neuroscience Research**. New Jersey. 2017. Available at <https://kesslerfoundation.org/researchcenter/nnl>. Accessed on: September 08, 2017.

MIX
Papier aus verantwortungsvollen Quellen
Paper from responsible sources
FSC® C105338

Printed by Books on Demand GmbH, Norderstedt / Germany